ENVIRONMENTAL ENGINEERING
AND THE Science of Sustainability

Vozilo na hibridni pogon

AURIS HYBRID

Crabtree Publishing Company
www.crabtreebooks.com

Robert Snedden

Crabtree Publishing Company

www.crabtreebooks.com

Author: Robert Snedden
Publishing plan research and development:
Reagan Miller
Project coordinator: Kathy Middleton
Photo research: James Nixon
Editors: Paul Humphrey, James Nixon,
Rachel Eagen
Proofreader: Wendy Scavuzzo
Layout: sprout.uk.com
Illustrations: sprout.uk.com
Cover design and logo: Margaret Amy Salter
Production coordinator and prepress technician: Tammy McGarr
Print coordinator: Margaret Amy Salter

Produced for Crabtree Publishing Company by Discovery Books

Photographs:
Alamy: pp. 7 (Justin Kasezninez), 10 (Aerial Archives), 13 (Michael Goulding/The Orange County Register/ZUMA Press, Inc.), 29 (Eddie Gerald).
Corbis: p. 9 (Hulton-Deutsch Collection).
Fondation d'entreprise Hermès: p. 25 (Gabriele Diamanti/DISKO).
NREL: p. 17 (Kenny Gruchalla & Matthew Churchfield).
Ramona du Houx: p. 15.
Shutterstock: cover, pp. 1 (ankiro), 1 left (Foto011), 1 top-right (xrphoto), 4 left (Alena Brozova), 4 right (Keith A Frith), 8 (Marques), 11 (falk), 12 (William Perugini), 16 (ankiro), 19 top (Goodluz), 19 bottom (Foto011), 20 (chevanon), 21 (spirit of america), 22 (hagit berkovich), 28 (Goodluz).
Wikimedia: pp. 6 (Hans Hillewaert/CC-BY-SA-3), 14 (James Provost).
www.lysekong.com: pp. 27 top, 27 bottom.

Library and Archives Canada Cataloguing in Publication

Snedden, Robert, author
    Environmental engineering and the science of sustainability / Robert Snedden.

(Engineering in action)
Includes index.
Issued in print and electronic formats.
ISBN 978-0-7787-1213-8 (bound).--ISBN 978-0-7787-1231-2 (pbk.).--ISBN 978-1-4271-8949-3 (pdf).--ISBN 978-1-4271-8945-5 (html)

    1. Environmental engineering--Juvenile literature.
2. Sustainability--Juvenile literature. I. Title. II. Series: Engineering in action (St. Catharines, Ont.)

TA170.S64 2013   j628   C2013-906151-7
    C2013-906152-5

Library of Congress Cataloging-in-Publication Data

Snedden, Robert.
 Environmental engineering and the science of sustainability / Robert Snedden.
    pages cm -- (Engineering in action)
 Audience: Ages 10-13.
 Audience: Grades 4 to 6.
 Includes index.
 ISBN 978-0-7787-1213-8 (reinforced library binding) -- ISBN 978-0-7787-1231-2 (pbk.) -- ISBN 978-1-4271-8949-3 (electronic pdf) -- ISBN 978-1-4271-8945-5 (electronic html)
 1. Environmental protection--Juvenile literature. 2. Environmental engineering--Juvenile literature. 3. Sustainable development--Juvenile literature. I. Title.

 TD170.15.S64 2014
 628--dc23
    2013035442

Crabtree Publishing Company

www.crabtreebooks.com   1-800-387-7650

Printed in the U.S.A./092014/CG20140808

Published in Canada
Crabtree Publishing
616 Welland Ave.
St. Catharines, ON
L2M 5V6

Published in the United States
Crabtree Publishing
PMB 59051
350 Fifth Avenue, 59th Floor
New York, New York 10118

Published in the United Kingdom
Crabtree Publishing
Maritime House
Basin Road North, Hove
BN41 1WR

Published in Australia
Crabtree Publishing
3 Charles Street
Coburg North
VIC, 3058

CONTENTS

PEOPLE AND PLANET

The better the quality of their surroundings, the healthier and happier people are. Finding ways of meeting people's needs while causing as little damage as possible to the **environment** is the job of environmental engineers.

Sustainable development

Earth's growing population makes many demands on the planet. We need a constant supply of resources such as food, fresh water, and safe, reliable sources of energy, to build and maintain our towns and cities. As resources are used to meet our needs today, environmental engineers find ways to ensure that the people living long after we are gone will also have a healthy environment and enough resources to enjoy their lives. This important idea is called **sustainable** development.

An environmental engineer tests a soil sample to check for dangerous chemicals.

What is the environment?: The environment is everything around you. It includes people and all the other living things you come into contact with, including bacteria, plants, and animals. It also includes non-living things, such as the water you drink, the air you breathe, the ground you walk on, and the materials used to build your home.

Like other engineers, environmental engineers follow an eight-step process when they are trying to design a solution to a problem (see diagram):

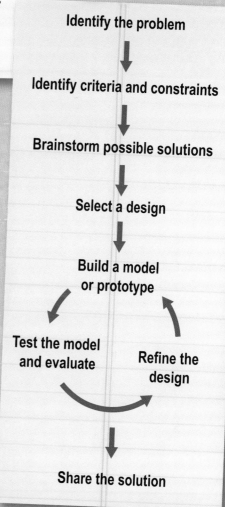

Identify the problem

↓

Identify criteria and constraints

↓

Brainstorm possible solutions

↓

Select a design

↓

Build a model or prototype

Test the model and evaluate

Refine the design

↓

Share the solution

ENGINEERING THE ENVIRONMENT

Environmental engineering is the practice of solving problems in a way that improves the quality of human life, while protecting the environment from the effects of human activities. Engineers must deal with problems relating to the environment at local and global levels. Among other things, environmental engineers find ways to keep water clean and control and manage **hazardous waste**. They look for energy sources that won't cause damaging changes, such as **global warming**, and they are involved in protecting wildlife. In many ways, environmental engineers might just be the most important engineers of all.

ENERGY ISSUES

More than 1.2 billion people in the world have no access to electricity. Around 2.8 billion people rely on fuels such as wood, coal, charcoal, and dung for heating and cooking. Every year, about 1.6 million people die of diseases caused by inhaling smoke and fumes from open fires. See page 11 to discover one way of supplying safer energy.

ENVIRONMENTAL ENGINEERS AT WORK

Environmental engineers do not just have to know how to design and make things—they also need the knowledge to understand how their work affects the environment. Environmental engineers are trained in the fields of **chemistry**, **biology**, **geology**, and **ecology**.

*The oceans are an important part of our environment. Environmental engineers monitor conditions in the oceans using equipment such as this **sensor**.*

GROWING DEMANDS

As more efforts are made to tackle environmental issues, the need for specialist engineers will grow. There are currently 1.5 million enviromental engineers in the United States, and their numbers are expected to grow quickly. There are predictions that Canada will face a shortage of environmental engineers soon.

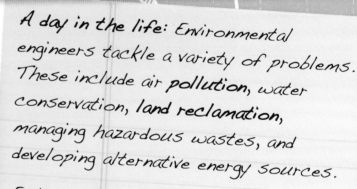

A day in the life: Environmental engineers tackle a variety of problems. These include air **pollution**, water conservation, **land reclamation**, managing hazardous wastes, and developing alternative energy sources.

Environmental engineers often work in teams. They consult with city planners about building sites, such as for new shopping malls. They also ensure that factories meet environmental regulations, including those dealing with **toxic** emissions.

CIVIL AND ENVIRONMENTAL ENGINEERING

Civil engineering is involved with the design and building of large structures, such as roads, bridges, and power plants. Environmental engineers combine civil engineering with environmental science. Both types of engineers tackle problems faced by society, such as how to transport goods, how to supply energy, and how to provide places for people to live and work. But environmental engineering also looks for ways to reduce the impact these activities have on the environment.

The Olympic Park built for the London 2012 Olympic Games was a huge project for environmental engineers. Recycled materials were used in its construction. It was powered by wind and solar power and aimed to produce zero waste for landfills.

Global impacts

Human activities can have an impact over a huge area. Wind and water can carry **pollutants** long distances, poisoning fish and other wildlife.

Global warming and **climate change** are a concern. Human activities, particularly burning **fossil fuels**, are believed to be contributing to an increase in average global temperatures by releasing **greenhouse gases**, which trap heat from Earth's surface that would otherwise escape into space. Environmental engineers are working to find alternative sources of energy that will reduce our use of fossil fuels and cut the amount of greenhouse gases we produce.

EARLY ENGINEERS

The Romans were among the greatest engineers of the ancient world. They designed complex systems that brought fresh water into their cities and carried away waste water and sewage.

The engineers of Rome

The **Aqueduct** of Segovia, built in modern-day Spain during the 1st century CE, is one of the most impressive examples of early environmental engineering. A system of stone channels brought fresh water from the Fuente Fria—a mountain river about 11 miles (18 km) away. The water flowed to the city from the force of **gravity** alone.

The aqueduct has 166 granite arches. Freshwater was delivered to public baths, **latrines**, fountains, and homes through a U-shaped channel in the upper level of the aqueduct. Dirty water and sewage was carried out in **sewers** built along the roadways. This wastewater was deposited in rivers and lakes far from the city.

The Roman Aqueduct of Segovia still stands in Segovia, Spain, but it is no longer in use.

Modern aqueducts

When the Brooks Aqueduct in Alberta was completed in 1914, it was the largest concrete structure of its kind in the world. Aqueducts are still used to carry fresh water. In the United States, the Catskill Aqueduct brings water from the Catskill Mountains to New York City, 120 miles (193 km) away, while the Central Arizona Project carries water from the Colorado River over 330 miles (531 km) to the cities of Phoenix and Tucson.

ENDING THE "GREAT STINK"

By the mid-19th century, the Thames River in London, England, was so badly polluted with raw sewage that the odor from it was nicknamed the Great Stink. The city hired engineer Joseph Bazalgette to come up with a solution. He designed a system of sewers that carried the polluted waters out of the city. Portions of his new sewer system are still part of London's waste management system today.

Bazalgette's work stopped the stink and also helped to prevent cholera—a fatal disease that is spread through water contaminated, or made impure, with bacteria. Today, environmental engineers commonly work with health-care professionals to keep people safe from diseases connected to pollution and other environmental problems.

Joseph Bazalgette inspects the construction of part of his new sewerage system.

SUSTAINABLE DEVELOPMENT

Long ago, it seemed as though there was an endless supply of the world's natural resources. Today, we know that there are limits to what we can use. Sustainable development means making sure that we use resources such as water, trees, and oil wisely, so they do not run out for future generations.

Enough for everyone: Sustainable development means finding ways to increase health and comfort for people today, while making sure there will also be enough resources for the future. The goal is to put practices in place that make sure there will always be enough for everyone.

The polluted air that hangs over cities such as Mexico City damages the health of the people who live there.

The engineer's role

Environmental engineers play a vital role in making sustainable development a reality. Through their work, they can help tackle the poverty and inequality that affect many of the world's people. As well as looking to the future, engineers find ways to fix past mistakes, such as inadequate water supply systems or inefficient use of energy sources.

Getting the job done

Engineers use their skills to design new tools or methods to get a job done. Environmental engineers look for ways to recycle resources, build more energy-**efficient** homes, improve transportation systems, and protect the environment. This will all have to be done as cheaply and conveniently as possible. It is a tough task!

SOLAR COOKERS

One engineering solution that is making life better is the solar cooker. This is a device that uses the free energy from the Sun to cook food. There are three types. The simplest is the box cooker—an insulated box with a transparent cover on top, which is lined with reflectors that help heat the box. Panel cookers use reflective panels to focus the Sun's heat onto a pot. Parabolic, or curved, cookers focus heat onto the bottom of the cooking pot. Parabolic cookers produce the highest temperatures.

Solar cookers like this one in India cook food cheaply, efficiently, and with none of the pollution that would come from a smoking fire.

MEETING THE ENERGY CHALLENGE

When our supplies of fossil fuels such as coal, oil, and gas were plentiful, few people worried about alternative sources of energy. Now we realize that not only are these fuels running out, but also that burning them may be damaging the environment.

The search for alternatives

The challenge of developing safe, sustainable energy is a massive problem, but it is one that environmental engineers will play a big part in solving. Just like other engineers, environmental engineers follow a series of steps to come up with the best solution.

Identify the problem: The first step the engineers have to take is to be sure they know exactly what the problem is. The fossil fuels that supply most of our energy needs are non-renewable resources. This means that the amount of fossil fuel is limited, and one day we will have used it all up. Environmental engineers want to find alternative sources of energy that are clean, reliable, and won't run out. One possible solution is to harness the power of the wind. What challenges do the engineers face in turning wind power into useful electricity?

Environmental engineers monitor the operation of the turbines on a wind farm.

Identify criteria and constraints: There are usually conditions that we must meet when solving a problem. These conditions are made up of criteria (the standards we want) and constraints (the limits on what we can actually do). The criteria for a wind-powered generator are likely to be that it is reasonably cheap to build and efficient to run. The constraints would include where to put it. The site would have to be windy, but away from places such as homes and airports. Wind turbines cannot be near radio and television transmitters, since they can interfere with the radio signal.

Brainstorming: The next step in the design process is to discuss different ways of making a wind-powered generator. The engineering team gets together and shares ideas in a brainstorming session. Everyone contributes to the discussion. Some of the suggestions might be totally impractical, but they could act as triggers for better ideas. The key to good brainstorming is to let the ideas flow without any criticism. This is a good way of coming up with different possible solutions to the problem.

In a brainstorming session, everyone involved has a chance to put forward their ideas.

DESIGNS AND PROTOTYPES

The best ideas from the brainstorming sessions will be sketched out as designs and plans that can be used to build models for testing.

Select a design: If all goes well, the brainstorming session should produce a number of useful ideas. Some of these might raise other problems that the team will need to work together to solve. How tall should the generator be? How will they make sure it faces into the wind? How big can the blades be? How strong must the mast, or post, be to support the blades?

The engineers will try out many different designs for their ideas, using both computer graphics and pencil and paper. They will work on the design until finally they agree that they have the best design for the wind turbine. Now it is time to move on to the next step— building a prototype.

One unusual design for a wind turbine is to have it suspended in the air, held up by a helium balloon. As the turbine spins, it generates electricity that is sent back down the tether to the ground.

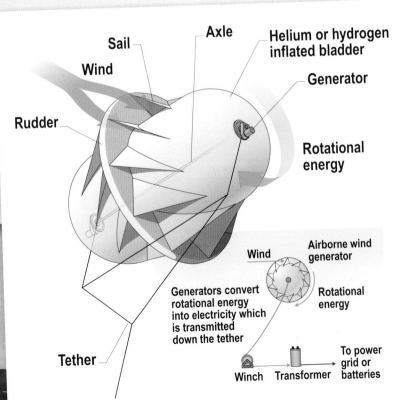

Sail

Wind

Rudder

Axle

Helium or hydrogen inflated bladder

Generator

Rotational energy

Tether

Wind

Airborne wind generator

Rotational energy

Generators convert rotational energy into electricity which is transmitted down the tether

Winch   Transformer

To power grid or batteries

Building and testing a prototype: A prototype is a first working model of a machine that can be tested in all possible ways to uncover any problems in the design. This is the engineers' chance to test how different components work together. They will look very carefully for flaws in the prototype. If it doesn't perform to their expectations, the engineers will then look again at the possible solutions they came up with when brainstorming and choose another model to build as a prototype. The engineers may have to test several different designs to find the one that works best.

Offshore testing

In June 2013, engineers from the United States Department of Energy and the University of Maine began testing a prototype offshore floating wind turbine.

The VolturnUS prototype is 65 feet (20 m) tall, but that is only one eighth the full size of the turbines that will be built if testing is successful. Offshore wind is a potentially huge source of energy. Floating turbines could be the answer to making this energy available for our use. By 2030, engineers hope to have about 170 full-sized turbines installed, each with blades longer than the wingspan of a Boeing 747. Each turbine will meet the electricity needs of around 2,000 homes.

This is the floating platform that supports the VolturnUS wind turbine. The yellow section is the part that stays above the water. Anchors hold the platform in position.

Refining the design: Using all the information they have gathered from testing their prototypes, the engineers make further changes to their design. When they are confident that they have the best possible solution to their problem, the engineers are ready to go into full-scale production.

ENGINEERING AND THE ENVIRONMENT

Unlike other engineers, environmental engineers aren't just looking for technical solutions to problems. They also have to be aware of the effects that an engineering project might have on the environment.

Environmental impacts

A large-scale construction project such as erecting a wind farm could affect the environment in several ways. For example, woodlands might have to be cleared to make room to build the turbines; water supplies could be disturbed or polluted by the digging of foundations to support the turbines; and wildlife could be endangered by the loss of habitat. On the positive side, replacing a fossil-fuel-burning power station with a wind farm cuts down on pollution. The list of all the good and bad effects that may result is called an environmental impact assessment. An assessment is an evaluation.

Working together

The environmental engineers consult with scientists and other engineers from many different fields to identify potential problems and to find solutions. For example, an ecologist will be able to advise on where to set up wind turbines so they will not be on the flight paths of migrating birds. A geologist can advise on whether sites are likely to have landslides, flooding, or earthquakes. An aerospace engineer can help fine-tune the design of the wind turbine's blades so they are as efficient as possible.

Wind turbines take up a small area on the ground, which means that other activities, such as farming, can continue around them.

Turbines capture the energy of the wind, so the wind speed is less behind them. Wind speeds of 30 miles per hour (48 km/h) may be reduced to 5 miles per hour (8 km/h) in the area behind each turbine (shown in blue). Computer modeling allows engineers to figure out how to position the turbines so the ones in front do not steal energy from the ones behind.

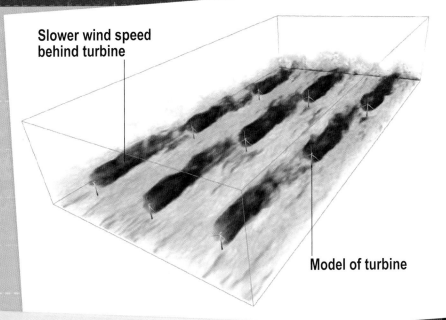

Slower wind speed behind turbine

Model of turbine

Computer modeling: Environmental engineers can use computer modeling to help with their impact assessments. In modeling, some aspect of the environment is recreated on the computer. The solutions the engineers came up with during brainstorming can all be tested on the virtual environment. This way, they can try out different solutions without affecting the actual environment. For example, a computer model might be used to try out different positions for the turbines on a wind farm to find the most effective placement.

Not so noisy

People often object to having wind farms built near their homes because they say that they are big, noisy, and unattractive. Like any other machine, a wind turbine does make some noise when it is working. Environmental engineers have continually improved the design of wind turbines to reduce the noise they make. Newer turbines are much quieter than earlier models. Reducing noise has the added benefit of making the turbine more energy efficient. The smoother the rotor turns, the less wind energy gets converted into annoying sound energy and the more goes into spinning the turbine and producing electricity.

ALTERNATIVE ENERGY ANSWERS

Wind power is not the only answer environmental engineers have come up with to help solve our energy problems. Here are a few more solutions that they are helping to develop.

Wave power

Waves are produced by the power of the wind blowing across the sea and they carry a considerable amount of energy. Environmental engineers are looking for ways to capture this energy and put it to use. The U.S. Electric Power Research Institute has estimated that enough electricity can be captured from waves around the coast of the United States to supply a third of the country's energy needs.

Solar power

The Sun generates more energy every day than the entire population of Earth uses in 30 years. Imagine if we could capture just a small part of that energy. Thanks to the work of engineers and scientists, we are getting better and better at doing just that. It is still more expensive to generate power from solar energy than it is from coal or gas, but that will change as solar energy technology improves and fossil fuels become scarcer and more expensive.

WATERY SOLUTION

One idea for harnessing wave power is the Oyster. The device is anchored to the seabed just offshore. Wave power pushes the Oyster back and forth, pumping water through a high-pressure pipe to drive a turbine onshore that produces electricity. Oysters are being used to supply power to thousands of homes in Scotland.

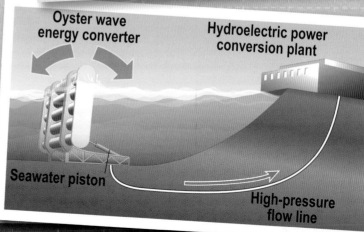

Oyster wave energy converter

Hydroelectric power conversion plant

Seawater piston

High-pressure flow line

Engineers meet on a rooftop to discuss the best places to locate banks of photovoltaic cells.

There are two ways of using solar energy. The simplest is to collect the Sun's heat. Solar thermal power plants use heat from the Sun to create steam, which is then used to spin turbines that generate electricity. On a smaller scale, solar thermal energy collectors on house roofs can heat water in homes. Solar cookers (see page 11) are another type of solar energy collector.

The second way of using solar energy relies on a device called a **photovoltaic cell**. A photovoltaic cell absorbs light and converts it directly into electricity. A solar panel is made up of a large number of photovoltaic cells working together. You might have seen them on the roofs of buildings or mounted on top of road signs. Environmental engineers and scientists are looking for ways to make these solar panels as efficient as possible. For example, they are developing ultra-thin, transparent materials that let as much light as possible through to the part of the cell that converts it into electricity.

Fuel economy

We can save energy by making sure we use what we have as economically as possible. A car that goes for many miles to the gallon is a good thing not only because it is more environmentally friendly, but also because it is cheaper to run. Environmental engineers are helping to achieve this by developing hybrid vehicles. A hybrid vehicle can run on both normal gas and on batteries. Engineers at Tufts University in Massachusetts are working on technology that could recharge the battery of a hybrid vehicle while it is being driven. The engineers' invention uses the motion of the vehicle to generate electricity, which is then used to recharge the battery.

Hybrid cars like this can run on environmentally friendly electric motors, as well as regular gas-powered engines.

WASTE MANAGEMENT

Our towns and cities produce thousands of tons of garbage every day. This solid waste can include everything from household garbage to old car tires, discarded computers, and the rubble from demolished buildings. This waste is another problem for environmental engineers to deal with.

Landfill sites

A great deal of solid waste is simply transported to large disposal sites called landfills. A landfill is like a huge garbage dump. Years ago, waste was simply dumped and left to rot. Today we are more aware of the problems that this can cause to the environment, such as the leaking of toxic chemicals into the soil and rivers. Environmental engineers have come up with ways to help prevent this.

Protecting the environment

Deciding where to place a landfill site is important. It shouldn't be near wetlands or rivers, or in areas where earthquakes are common. The bottom and sides of the landfill site are formed from a layer of compacted clay soil. This is then covered with a sheet of plastic. Water that drains through the waste picks up toxic chemicals. This contaminated water is called leachate. The plastic liner stops leachate from escaping into the surrounding soil. A system of pipes collects the leachate and carries it to treatment plants where it can be disposed of safely.

Untreated landfill sites, such as this one in Thailand, don't just look bad, they can also release dangerous chemicals into the environment.

Waste energy

The methane gas produced by materials that are breaking down in a landfill site can be collected through a series of pipes. The gas can then be burned to produce electricity. Some wastes are **incinerated** directly to produce electricity. The U.S. Environmental Protection Agency determined that incinerating one ton of waste produces 10 times more electricity than burying it and capturing the methane.

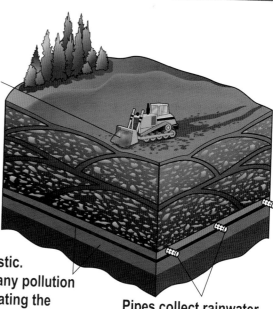

Each day's garbage is covered with a layer of soil.

The site has a clay base and is lined with heavy plastic. This prevents any pollution from contaminating the water in the ground and soil.

Pipes collect rainwater and any liquid waste.

Improved design of landfill sites allows toxic chemicals to be collected and treated.

Reuse, recycle

Another way to manage waste is to reduce how much we produce in the first place. In the United States, around one third of solid waste is recycled, including half the aluminum cans produced and nearly three-quarters of newspapers and printed material.

Sorting out waste for recycling can be done in a variety of ways. Machines can separate out materials by size and weight, and powerful electromagnets can lift out iron and steel. However, a lot of the sorting still has to be done by hand. Perhaps designing a fully automated waste sorting process is a job for a future environmental engineer.

Removing unwanted materials and sorting plastics and glass into different types still has to be done by hand at the recycling center.

SAFE WATER

Keeping our supplies of fresh water safe is tremendously important. Sustainable development of water resources, water supplies, and wastewater treatment is another major task facing environmental engineers.

Finding water

Fresh water may be found as surface water in rivers and lakes, or as **groundwater** trapped underground in rocks and soil. Engineers have to drill into the ground and use pumps to bring groundwater to the surface.

Water pressure: Around 1.1 billion of the world's people do not have easy access to water, while 2.7 billion find water hard to get for at least one month of the year. Lack of water makes poor **sanitation** a potential problem for 2.4 billion people.

Children use a pump to obtain groundwater from a well.

OUR WATERY PLANET

Seven tenths of Earth is covered by ocean, but only three percent of Earth's water is fresh water, and only one percent of that is available to us. The rest is frozen in ice caps and glaciers.

Water treatment

Water has to be treated before it is safe to drink. Surface water may contain disease-causing **microorganisms**, while harmful chemicals may contaminate groundwater. Environmental engineers have developed ways of treating water to make it safe for us to drink. The treatment process involves three steps: clarification, filtration, and disinfection. Clarification means removing larger particles of soil and other materials. Heavier particles settle to the bottom and lighter particles can be skimmed off the surface. Filtration means filtering out even smaller particles by passing the water through sand or carbon filters. Disinfection usually means adding chlorine, which kills any bacteria and viruses in the water.

Environmental engineers set up networks of pipes, treatment plants, and storage areas to make sure we have a reliable supply of clean water.

Supply system

Treated water then has to be delivered to where it is needed. This means designing and building a pumping system. The engineers designing the system must take into account factors such as the materials used to make the pipes (they must be long-lasting and not likely to release undesirable chemicals into the water) and how the system can expand in the future to meet increasing demands.

Wastewater

As with other scarce resources, we must recycle as much water as possible. Wastewater from homes and industries is sent through sewers to water treatment plants. Harmful pollutants are removed there, and the water is returned to the environment.

DESIGN CHALLENGE: DESALINATION PROJECT

Most of the world's water supply is undrinkable salt water from the world's oceans. But environmental engineers can make it drinkable by building equipment that removes the salt in a process called **desalination**. Worldwide, 16 billion gallons of fresh water are produced by desalination every day.

1: The problem: Find a way to separate salt from water.

2: Criteria and constraints: You will need a container to hold the salt water and another to collect the fresh water. You will have to prevent the fresh water from mixing back into the salt water.

3: Brainstorm solutions: How will you make the water evaporate? And how will you collect the evaporated water? Can you make it drip into another container, or can you find a way of soaking it up?

There are desalination plants in many coastal areas producing fresh water for people and agriculture. It's easy enough to do. The water is allowed to **evaporate**, leaving the salt behind. The trickiest part is trapping the evaporated water. How would you go about making a small desalination plant of your own?

This is just one possibility for a desalination plant. Your ideas may be much better!

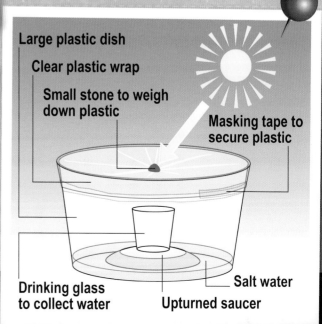

Large plastic dish

Clear plastic wrap

Small stone to weigh down plastic

Masking tape to secure plastic

Drinking glass to collect water

Upturned saucer

Salt water

4: Decide on your design: Try to bring all your ideas together in a design. As you sketch your design, identify all the equipment that you'll need.

5: Build a prototype: This is just an idea to get you started. Add a little salt to some clean water. Pour this salt water into a large bowl and place an empty glass, open side up, in the center. If the glass falls over, do you think you will have more success with a heavier or lighter one? Cover the bowl, including the empty glass, with plastic wrap. A small weight in the middle will help the water drip into the glass.

6: Test the prototype: Leave your desalination plant for a few hours while it does its work. The water should evaporate, then form into water drops on the plastic wrap and drip into the empty glass.

Italian designer Gabriele Diamanti designed this simple, portable desalination plant.

7: Make improvements: Will it make any difference if the salt water is in a wide, shallow container or in a tall, narrow one? Will it work better in warm or cool conditions? (Think about puddles. Do they evaporate faster on warm days or cold ones?) Can you think of a better way to collect the fresh water?

8: Communicate: Invite someone to drink the water you've collected in the glass to show them (and you) that your desalination plant has worked. It should be salt-free and perfectly drinkable!

PREPARING FOR TOMORROW

The major challenges facing environmental engineers in the 21st century are climate change, making the best use of our limited resources, and meeting the needs of a growing population. Dealing with these problems will take a lot of teamwork among engineers and scientists with a wide range of skills and knowledge.

A nuclear solution?

One possibile way to cut down on the amount of fossil fuels we use would be to have more nuclear power plants. Many people are against this because they worry that hazardous nuclear waste could be released into the air or water during accidents. Others think nuclear power could, if safely controlled, be a major part of the battle to stop global warming. Environmental engineers at Imperial College in London, England, are designing nuclear power plant assembly kits. Large, reinforced concrete parts can be manufactured and sent to the site of a new power plant to be put together there. Assembling the parts onsite will mean less disruption to the surrounding area from construction and should also mean less waste is created. Researchers will carry out tests to make sure the parts meet strict safety standards for power plant construction.

Cooling sprays

One idea for cooling the planet is to build floating machines that shoot droplets of ocean water into the air, thickening clouds so they reflect more of the solar energy that warms Earth back into space. These "spray ships" could suck up 10 tons of seawater a second and blast it 3,280 feet (1 km) into the air. However, even the developers admit that it would take a fleet of nearly 2,000 ships to bring down Earth's temperature.

A fleet of ships spraying water into the atmosphere is one of the more imaginative proposals to fight global warming.

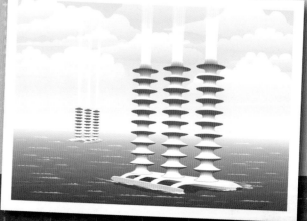

Small beginnings

Often the way to tackle big environmental problems is to start on a small scale. A portable desalination device (see page 25) is simple to make, but can improve life for millions of people. Environmental engineers are working to develop other technologies like this. To make sustainable development a reality, we need devices that are easy to build, easy to run, and effective at what they do.

Cleaner fuel

People in many parts of the world make charcoal for fuel. But charcoal can also be used to filter harmful pesticides and other chemicals from water. Josh Kearns, an engineer from the University of Colorado-Boulder, has been working with people in Thailand to produce the best charcoal for water treatment. He has developed burners called gasifiers that can be run on agricultural and forestry wastes, such as corn stalks and tree branches. Best of all, the design of the gasifiers is so simple that anyone can make one, not just engineering experts! These produce far less pollution than traditional charcoal burners, and the heat they give off can be used for cooking and for drying crops.

Engineer Josh Kearns is shown operating a gasifier with a Thai farmer. Gasifiers operate at a higher temperature than ordinary charcoal ovens and produce charcoal much more quickly.

The gasifier must reach temperatures of 1,380°F–1,740°F (749°C–949°C). Producing charcoal that can be used for water treatment depends on reaching these high temperatures.

27

SO YOU WANT TO BE AN ENVIRONMENTAL ENGINEER?

The need for environmental engineers isn't going to go away any time soon—their skills will always be in demand. If you want to be an environmental engineer, you'll have to be able to think on both large and small scales.

Students on a field trip discuss the problems of ensuring a safe water supply.

An engineer's life: Environmental engineer Yvana Kuhn is a keen scuba diver and takes a particular interest in the coastal environment. An American Council of Engineering Companies "Young Professional of the Year," Yvana sees water resource management as one of our greatest challenges. "I enjoy thinking on my feet and working on challenging projects that require creative solutions," she says. Her job has taken her around the world to work on projects in Hawaii, China, and the United Arab Emirates.

You should be able to come up with inventive solutions to problems, making good use of the materials available. You'll need an understanding of scientific principles in biology, chemistry, physics, and computer science. It helps if you enjoy being outdoors, too.

People power

Environmental engineering projects are carried out with people in mind. Managing hazardous waste, studying the impact of building a factory, or helping reduce the effects of global warming, all affect people. As an environmental engineer, you'll need good communication skills to explain what you're doing and get people on your side.

After the 2010 earthquake in Haiti, people had to find their own water as best they could. Environmental engineers are trying to help prevent such shortages in future disasters.

Engineers to the rescue

Environmental engineers may be called on to act as part of the team dealing with a natural disaster. When Haiti was devastated by an earthquake in 2010, people were in desperate need of clean water and power.

Engineers from Princeton University decided to develop technology that would help in future disaster relief. First, they developed a rainwater harvester. This uses pot-shaped water filters made from easy-to-find materials, such as clay and sawdust. When the filters are heated and dried in a kiln, or oven, the sawdust burns away, leaving tiny holes that let clean water flow through but not harmful bacteria. The second project was a wind turbine designed to be set up quickly in a disaster area to provide emergency power for a hospital, school, or homes. The Princeton team are also creating a map of Haiti's wind energy resources to find the most promising sites for wind turbines.

LEARNING MORE

BOOKS

Agnieszka Biskup, *The Incredible Work of Engineers with Max Axiom, Super Scientist*, Capstone Press, 2013

Mary Colson, *From Fail to Win! Learning From Bad Ideas: The Environment*, Raintree, 2011

Suzy Gazlay, *Re-greening the Environment*, Crabtree Publishing, 2011

Mike Hobbs, *Green Technology*, Smart Apple Media, 2013

Seymour Simon, *Global Warming*, HarperCollins, 2013

Louise Spilsbury, *Can the Earth Cope?: Water Supply*, Wayland, 2013

ONLINE

http://ga.water.usgs.gov/edu/
The USGS *Water Science School: all about water and the ways we use it.*

http://www.ec.gc.ca
Discover how the Canadian government is working to protect the environment.

www.discoverengineering.org
Explore the world of engineering, including environmental engineering, and see how engineers can change the world.

www.engineeryourlife.org/cms/Careers/
Descriptions/Environmental.aspx
Think environmental engineering might be your dream job? Find out more about it here.

www.epa.gov/climatestudents
A student's guide to the causes and effects of, and possible solutions to, climate change.

www.jobshadow.com/interview-with-an-environmental-engineer
Interview with an environmental engineer

PLACES TO VISIT

Canada Science and Technology Museum, Ottawa:
www.sciencetech.technomuses.ca
Find out about the links between technology and society, as well as recent advances in managing renewable resources.

Museum of Science and Industry, Chicago: www.msichicago.org
Learn how to use a solar oven, make a wind turbine, and see how technology has transformed farming.

Museum of Science, Boston: www.mos.org
See the turbines at work in the Wind Lab, learn about other safe, renewable sources of energy, and much more.

National Building Museum, Washington, DC: www.nbm.org
Discover the architectural, engineering, and design skills that are used to build the places we live in.

GLOSSARY

aqueduct A pipe or channel built to carry water from one place to another

biology The scientific study of living things

chemistry The scientific study of substances and their properties and the ways in which they react with each other

climate change The change in Earth's average weather over time, especially that caused by global warming

desalination The removal of salt from water to make it suitable for drinking

ecology The branch of biology that studies how living things interact with each other and with their environment

efficient Something that produces maximum results with the minimum wasted effort

environment The surroundings or conditions in a place, including all the living and non-living things found there

evaporate To turn from a liquid into a vapor without boiling

fossil fuels Fuels that formed from the ancient remains of plants and animals that lived millions of years ago; coal, petroleum, and natural gas are fossil fuels

geology The study of the structure of Earth

global warming A rise in the average temperature of Earth, believed by most scientists to result from rising levels of greenhouse gases in the atmosphere

gravity The force of attraction between objects, such as Earth and the moon, or Earth and an apple; gravity is what makes a ball thrown into the air fall back downward

greenhouse gases Gases in the atmosphere, such as carbon dioxide, methane, or water vapor, that trap heat that would otherwise escape into space

groundwater Water held under the ground in soil and rocks

hazardous waste Waste that may be a danger to the environment and to people's health

incinerated Destroyed by burning

land reclamation The conversion of wasteland into land that can be used for agriculture or construction

latrine A type of toilet

microorganisms Living things that are too small to see without a microscope

photovoltaic cell A device that converts light energy into electrical energy

pollutants Unwanted, often harmful, chemicals found in the environment

pollution The presence in the environment of substances that may have harmful effects

sanitation Measures that safeguard public health, particularly through the provision of fresh water and the safe disposal of wastes

sensor A device used to detect and measure something, such as noise or the presence of a chemical

sewers Pipes for carrying off rainwater or wastewater

sustainable Able to be maintained at a certain rate or level

toxic Poisonous

INDEX